MARY ANNING of LYME REGIS

Crispin Tickell

Published by Lyme Regis Philpot Museum

ISBN 0 9527662 0 5

First Published 1996
Reprinted 1998

Acknowledgements
The Museum would like to thank Jo Draper for her help in producing the book; Dr Robert Allison for providing the photograph of Black Ven for the cover; and Dr Hugh Torrens for leading us to the illustration on p 25.

Cover design by Valerie Baker, with acknowledgement to the Natural History Museum for the figure of Mary Anning, taken from the portrait reproduced on p 6.

Printed by Sherrens, Units 1 & 2, South Park, Granby Industrial Estate, Weymouth DT4 9YX

FOREWORD

'Mary Anning, probably the most important unsung (or inadequately sung) collecting force in the history of palaeontology ... made an astounding series of discoveries, including squidlike creatures with associated ink-bags, a plesiosaur in 1824, and a pterosaur (flying reptile) in 1828. She directly found, or pointed the way to, nearly every specimen of importance.'

Finders, Keepers. Stephen Jay Gould, Pimlico 1992

Gould is perhaps the best-known biologist and historian of science in America. The great expert on Mary Anning here is the geologist and similarly learned historian of geology, Dr Hugh Torrens. Readers who want a full academic account of her must await his biography. We are meanwhile exceptionally fortunate to have this perceptive view of her from someone who is not only in his own right a distinguished diplomat and the present head of Green College at Oxford but is actually descended from Mary's elder brother, Joseph. Earlier this century two of Sir Crispin Tickell's great-aunts were respectively secretaries to the famous Victorian crusading journalist W T Stead and to no less a pugnacious politician than Winston Churchill. I fancy Mary would have recognised a kindred spirit there, in both them and their employers.

It really does need a very considerable leap of the imagination to grasp the extent to which early nineteenth-century Dorset - and indeed much elsewhere in Britain - was severely constricted, almost imprisoned, by an innocence of language, most obviously in the prevalence of dialect. Neither Mary nor her brother - or indeed their mother, also Mary or Molly - would have been at all at home with a normal educated (or modern 'received') accent. Full Dorset accents began to disappear around Lyme about 1900. At a parliamentary hustings at the very beginning of this century one would-be gentleman candidate was questioned. 'And who might you be?' the candidate asked. The reply became immortal in local folklore. The old fellow proudly said, 'Zurr, Oi be a Darrset man.' For ever afterwards he was nicknamed 'I-be-a-Dorset-man'. By that time strong accents were already risible, and their associated ways of thinking distinctly oldfashioned.

Lyme was always rather more prone to lose (or 'bury') its old voices because of the constant influx of holiday-makers from abroad - anywhere more than ten miles from Lyme - in summer. We call them grockles in local slang nowadays. This 'other' Lyme, the one formed by external visitors, began about 1760, when we have a first bill recording the painting of some bathing-machines. Grockles now outnumber natives by some five to six to one every high summer, but the Dorset accent was still heavy enough in the 1880s to warrant study.

Mary's father may have stumbled on the profits to be got from collecting 'curios' mainly through his contacts with Charmouth. The London to Exeter stage coaches stopped there, but avoided the steep hills down to Lyme. He died in 1811 and for a time Mary senior and her two children were 'on the parish'. But by 1820 they had a great stroke of good fortune, at least partly because of the assiduity of both mother and children. Although it is hard to see Mary as born more than a poor artisan's daughter, she was to become increasingly acquainted with better-to-do people, like the famous geologists Buckland and De la Beche, and perhaps above all with three sisters who came to Lyme about 1806, when Mary was seven. All three sisters Philpot - especially the longest-lived, Elizabeth - were truly serious collectors, and evidently soon took the dead carpenter's daughter under their wing. (Their important collection is now the foundation of that at Oxford University.)

What seems apparent is that despite her earlier social and educational disadvantages almost all the important palaeontologists, both amateur and professional, and their wives happily accepted her imperfections in view of her truly brilliant talent both for finding and preparing unusual, sometimes then unknown, specimens. Mary was evidently no beauty, and could be in the old Dissenting tradition distinctly forthright. She was highly successful both as a commercial fossil-seller and a cliff and foreshore guide, with a shrewd business sense. Both her later shop in Broad Street and her general advice were widely visited and sought. Yet despite this she never married.

In many ways she remains something of an enigma, a self-taught woman who still stayed very nearly working-class in countless ordinary ways. She does not seem to have fitted too well into Lyme, which has, or had, the sharpest nose in the world for all who dare to rise above their station. In her last years she was accused of drinking, though the truth is much sadder. She had cancer of the breast. No doubt, like so many Victorian women, she took laudanum to ease the pain.

Most previous biographers have wanted, for reasons of their own, to foist other personalities on her. One is purely romantic, the presumption of some secret sexual passion or affaire in her life. Colonel Birch (who did greatly help her family when in need) and Henry Thomas De la Beche (a fine geologist, who definitely knew her well when both were young in Lyme) are the usual men chosen to play the Heathcliff role. A great deal has been unearthed of Mary's professional and business correspondence; but alas, not a single one of the kind that today's sentimental limpets crave. Another costume she has often been forced into is that of the early feminist. But apart from Wollstonecraft, the earliest serious political stirrings of feminism began several years after Mary's death in 1847. The suffragettes were hardly significant before the 1890s.

If Mary was born with a chip on her shoulder, as the Anna Maria Pinney diaries hint, and which perhaps explain a later pride in her own celebrity that amounted almost to arrogance, the final conclusion of all of us who have studied her must remain as Gould suggests in the initial quotation. Beneath whatever physical ordinariness, whatever flaws in grammar, spelling and *savoir-vivre,* whatever roughnesses she may have shown, a truly remarkable human being for her epoch stood and stands behind.

By an odd coincidence a girl from fashionable Bath holidayed at Lyme in 1818 and wrote a long mock-epic poem about the town. She dedicates it to an imaginary Lymia, 'the genius of this shore'. Lymia wore a belt of shells, her hair was elegantly wreathed with sea-weed and on her head sat a diadem of ammonites. The anonymous poetess call her 'a strange fantastic figure'; alas, 1818 predates Mary Anning's first fame and I think cannot refer to her. The *Lymiad* is as yet unpublished, but exhibits a very Austen-like dryness (affectionate yet sharp) about the provinciality of the place. However, just such a figure, if far less picturesquely garbed, could certainly have been seen on Lyme's shores in 1818. Lyme does now elect a beauty queen every summer, but if we were ever to have to choose one to stand its eternal winner, it would be the subject of this essay. I am truly delighted that it is both a man and a descendant who so scrupulously and richly repays such a now long-owed debt from his historically male-monopolized science.

John Fowles, 1995

Portrait in oil of Mary Anning by Grey, 1841, reproduced by courtesy of the Natural History Museum. The portrait was given to the museum by Annette Anning, a great aunt of the author.

Mary Anning of Lyme Regis

Lyme Regis is built on the prolific remains of English history. There is an ancient sea wall like a prong into the bay. Above it and to the east stretch houses in a curve along the front as far as the mouth of the Buddle or river Lym. The main street upwards follows a natural contour. On three sides the town is enclosed by hills and crumbling cliffs, and on the fourth it looks towards the sea. Over centuries trade gave it prosperity and a radical tradition. Lyme has always combined openness with a strong sense of itself.

Mary Anning, daughter of a cabinet maker or carpenter, was born on 21 May 1799, ten years before Charles Darwin. Through her discoveries of creatures from a past vastly greater than anything she or her contemporaries can have imagined, she came to embody the open, radical and independent traditions of Lyme, and to contribute to an intellectual revolution whose effects are with us still.

Almost 200 million years ago the place which is now Lyme was a somewhat muddy sea not far from land at around 40° of latitude. In a warm climate organic matter washed into stagnant depths similar to parts of the Black Sea and the Mediterranean today. Life was already prolific. At the bottom of the food chain were plankton and such filter-feeders as oysters, crinoids and barnacles; a rich variety of cephalopods or marine molluscs, including belemnites and many species of ammonite (far distant cousins of the present day nautilus); and at the top many species of fish and such carnivores and scavengers as big marine or airborne reptiles: ichthyosaurs, plesiosaurs, pliosaurs and pterodactyls. When they died the remains of these creatures gradually fell to the murky bottom where for lack of oxygen many were preserved, and over millions of years subjected to enormous pressures and in many cases petrification. Today they are found among the geological formations, notably the Blue Lias, which run like fillings in a sandwich exposed in the cliffs along the west Dorset coast.

Of course fossils, and in particular these fossils, had been known for generations. For a world in which time was compressed by the supposed chronology of the Old Testament, and creation of different species had happened once and for all for human benefit, they were an embarrassing mystery, best if not fully explained by the Flood. It was for example hard to account for marine fossils found on mountain tops. A Jesuit scholar of the seventeenth century interpreted them as manifestations of a plastic force inherent in rocks, and a few even believed that they were left around by God as a test of faith. Until the mid-nineteenth century many thought that living specimens of fossil species could be found somewhere in the world if only people looked hard enough for them. In Dorset they were lumped together as dragons, crocodiles, ladies fingers or curios. For the most part they were simply admired as curiosities but were scarcely intelligible within most people's frames of reference.

Into this world came Mary Anning, the second surviving child of Richard and Molly Anning (born Mary Moore of Blandford).* Richard Anning probably emigrated from Colyton in Devon to Lyme Regis to take advantage of the rising prosperity of the town as a seaside resort on a new turnpike road. There is a tantalizing reference to him in a letter written by Jane Austen to her sister Cassandra on 14 September 1804, when he was brought in to value a broken lid (she thought his estimate of five shillings was 'beyond the value of all the furniture in the room together': perhaps he was simply trying to get what could be got out of visitors to Lyme).

Richard Anning was a dissenter, a recognized 'character', and no friend of the ruling establishment. In 1800 he was identified as one of the ringleaders of a destructive mob which rioted at a time of

* For the account which follows of Mary Anning and her family, I am indebted to W D Lang for his pioneer work recorded in articles, pamphlets and private correspondence; and particularly to Hugh Torrens who has brought much new material together, notably in his Presidential Address to the British Society for the History of Science (BSHS) in April, 1993, published in the *British Journal for the History of Science*, Vol 28, pp 257 - 284, 1995.

acute local food shortages. It seems that from the beginning he supplemented his income by selling fossils, sometimes gathered when the Anglican faithful were in church, from a table in front of his shop by the Cockmoil prison. (The Anning house and shop were on the site of the present Museum.) In later years Mary apparently said, perhaps with more filial piety than truth, that she was indebted to her father for all the knowledge she had about fossils. As a little girl she and her elder brother Joseph (1796 - 1849) certainly accompanied him on his expeditions.

Richard thereby initiated what became a modest family business. Although his wife Molly (*c* 1764 - 1842), apparently another 'original', began by finding fossil-collecting ridiculous, she soon came to think otherwise, and remained involved until her death. Joseph was likewise involved, at least until he left to become a full time upholsterer in 1825. It was probably Joseph who in 1811 discovered the head of the famous 'crocodile' to which Mary and he attached the rest of the skeleton after excavating it a year later. Although this was not the first Ichthyosaur to be found (as popular legend had it), it was a specimen which attracted widespread interest, and now occupies an honoured place in the Natural History Museum in London.

Richard Anning died in 1810, the result of consumption and of injuries caused by a fall when taking a short cut across Black Ven, then as now one of the most fossiliferous but dangerous cliffs near Lyme. He left his family destitute, and from 1811 to at least 1815 his widow and children were on poor relief. The sale of the Ichthyosaur to the Lord of the Manor Henry Henley for £23 (a large sum in those days) must greatly have helped the family finances. It also seemed to stimulate interest in fossils and fossil gathering. From 1817 onwards we hear of the activities of other collectors, especially the three Philpot sisters, who, often with Mary Anning's help, put together a remarkable collection, now in the Oxford University Museum.

By 1818, another more complete Ichthyosaur had been found. It was acquired by Thomas James Birch (1768 - 1829). In March 1820 he wrote to the enthusiastic fossilist and doctor Gideon Mantell that he was planning to sell his collection

> ... for the benefit of the poor woman (Molly Anning) and her son (Joseph) and daughter (Mary) at Lyme who have in truth found almost *all* the fine things, which have been submitted to scientific investigation: when I went to Charmouth & Lyme last summer (1819) I found these people in considerable difficulty - in the act of selling their furniture to pay their rent - in consequence of their not having found one good fossil for near a twelve month.[1]

When the sale took place in May that year, it attracted a lot of buyers, including from across the Channel, and raised over £400. The Birch/Anning Ichthyosaur alone went for £100. Other specimens went to the French naturalist George Cuvier.

By then the Annings were well known, and Mary especially among them. Her infancy had been marked by a dramatic incident. Until the age of fifteen months she was 'in a very weak state of health'. Her nurse or carer Elizabeth Haskings took her to an exhibition of riders in a field near the town. There was a thunderstorm of exceptional violence. A flash of lightning struck the elm under which Elizabeth Haskings and two women with her were sheltering, and killed all of them. When people pulled Mary Anning from the burnt body of Elizabeth Haskings, they found her alive but unconscious. She was revived in warm water, and in the words of Elizabeth's widower twenty year later she

> ... soon recovered, and from that time ... got better health, the physicians say the shock the Child received must be like that from a Lecturefing Machine, it may be said the death of the Nurse was the life of the Child.[2]

Mary Anning's nephew Charles Anning described the incident, by then family folklore, in 1847:

> She had been a dull child before but after this accident she became lively and intelligent, and grew up so.[3]

Recognition of Mary's qualities is all the more remarkable when she is seen in the context of her times. She came from a poor dissenting artisan family, and, so far as is known, had no formal education after the death of her father when she was eleven. She must have spoken in a heavy Dorset accent. She never married at a time when women were generally expected to do so. Throughout her life she maintained a solitary independence of spirit. She worked for money - in short she was no lady - and did the best deals she could in selling her discoveries. Most of her letters and papers which have survived relate to her business. She wrote in idiosyncratic style, spelling and grammar, but could use a telling phrase (for example sending 'a mouthful of new years kisses' to her friend Miss Lister in 1840).

Above all she was a woman in a man's world. Science was still largely the province of the leisured gentleman amateur. His role, and sometimes that of his lady, was to put together collections of objects - whether minerals, wild flowers, sea shells or fossils - without either of them getting mud up their finger nails or acknowledging the role of those who had done the hard work beforehand. Moreover Mary Anning was working in a dangerous area. Her discoveries had worrying if not subversive implications at a time of social turmoil which made people cling all the harder to familiar religious beliefs and the established order.

Comments on her were often double edged. On 25 October 1831 the youthful Anna Maria Pinney wrote in her journal:

> Went out at 11 o'clock fossilizing with Mary Anning. She is a woman of low birth, her brother is an upholsterer here, and one of William's (her brother's) voters.... She has been noticed by all the cleverest men in England, who have her to stay at their houses, correspond with her on geology etc. This has completely turned her head, and she has the proudest and most unyielding spirit I have ever met with. Much 'learning has made her mad'. She glories in being afraid of no one and in saying everything she pleases. She would offend all the world, were she not considered a privileged person.[4]

Across the class divide this counts for admiration. In fact she had attracted the attention of the local gentry even during her teens; and Henry De la Beche (elected to the Royal Society in 1819, knighted in 1848 and first Director of the Geological Survey) was her regular companion on the Lyme Regis beaches. Interested or learned visitors came increasingly from far and wide - William Buckland, William Conybeare, Sir Philip Egerton, Lord Enniskillen,

Louis Agassiz, even the King of Saxony - to look at her specimens or draw upon her wisdom. Eventually she became as much of an attraction as the fossils she sold from her tiny shop in Broad Street, now demolished.

In the early 1820's Molly Anning was still running the business, but Mary seems gradually to have taken over from her. In 1823 George Cumberland reported on her particular role in finding 'the finest specimen of a Fossil Ichthyosaurus'. He added in a footnote

> This persevering female has for years gone daily in search of fossil remains of importance at every tide, for many miles under the hanging cliffs of Lyme, whose fallen masses are her immediate object, as they alone contain these valuable relics of a former world, which must be snatched at the moment of their fall, at the continual risk of being crushed by the half suspended fragments they leave behind, or be left to be destroyed by the returning tide; - to her exertions we owe nearly *all* the fine specimens of Ichthyosauri of the great collections ...[5]

In the following year, when Mary was only 25, Thomas Allan the mineralogist commented on her surprising knowledge:

> ... she is perfectly acquainted with the anatomy of her subjects, and her account of her disputes with Buckland, whose anatomical science she holds in great contempt, was quite amusing.[6]

Lady Silvester also found her extraordinary when she visited her on 17 September 1824:

> ... It is certainly a wonderful instance of divine favour - that this poor, ignorant girl should be so blessed, for by reading and application she has arrived to that degree of knowledge as to be in the habit of writing and talking with professors and other clever men on the subject, and they all acknowledge that she understands more of the science than anyone else in the kingdom.[7]

For his part George William Featherstonehaugh, an American geologist and customer of Mary Anning's in 1827, described her as 'a very clever, funny Creature'. Not all were equally admiring.

Duria Antiquior *or* Ancient Dorsetshire, *a lively representation of the fauna and flora of the Liassic period in a sketch by De la Beche of 1830. The illustration, from a colour-tinted lithograph in one of R I Murchison's Notebooks, is reproduced by kind permission of the Department of Geology of the National Museum of Wales.*

Gideon Mantell called on her on 27 June 1832:

> After taking refreshment and washing, we sallied out in quest of Mary Anning, the geological Lioness of the place. We found her in a little dirty shop, with hundreds of specimens piled around, and in the greatest disorder. She, the presiding Deity, a prim, pedantic vinegar looking, thin female, shrewd and rather satirical in her conversation.[8]

Perhaps she had been satirical at Gideon Mantell's expense. When the King of Saxony visited her on 1 July 1844, his physician wrote afterwards

> ... the woman who kept the shop - for it was a woman who had devoted herself to this scientific pursuit - with a firm hand wrote her name, 'Mary Annins' in my pocket book, and added, as she returned the book into my hands, 'I am well known throughout the whole of Europe'.[9]

This apparently arrogant remark may have concealed two sore points. Throughout her life Mary Anning must have felt that she got relatively little credit for her discoveries. As Anna Maria Pinney wrote in her journal on 25 October 1831

> ... She says the world has used her ill and she does not care for it, according to her account these men of learning have sucked her brains, and made a great deal by publishing works, of which she furnished the contents, while she derived none of the advantages ...[10]

Until recently almost none of her discoveries displayed in museums or collections in different parts of the world carried her name. Instead they carried that of the donors. To establish her role today as discoverer usually requires research among secondary sources. She wrote no learned papers for scholarly archives, and was rarely if ever mentioned in them until long after her death (and as it is well known, academics find it hard to believe anything which is not written down). During her lifetime only two of the species she had identified were named after her, and those were by the great Swiss scientist Louis Agassiz. Some may have believed this unfair, even at the time. She obviously felt it strongly.

She must also have resented her anomalous situation in a society as stratified as the Lyme Regis cliffs. She never attempted to cut herself off from her origins, or to pretend that she was other than what she was. But she increasingly enjoyed the attentions and company of the learned, rich and well born of her day. By them she was treated with respect, not as one of them, but as someone special in her own right. She could even afford to laugh at them. Thus in a letter to Lady Murchison, probably written in 1828, she said 'I do so enjoy an opposition among the big-wigs'.[11] In the words of Anna Maria Pinney on 25 October 1831

> She says she stands still, and the world flows by her in a stream, that she likes observing it and discovering the different characters which compose it. But in discovering these characters, she takes most violent likes and dislikes... Associating and being courted by those above her, she frankly owns that the society of her own rank is become distasteful to her, but yet she is very kind and good to all her own relations, and what money she gets by collecting fossils, goes to them or to anyone else who wants it.[12]

In those days the upwardly mobile needed at least two or three generations before coming to rest at a new level.

This raises an interesting question which has caused much speculation, especially among authors of children's books about her. It has become an assumption that everyone must have a sex life. So time and trouble has been taken to show that Mary Anning had one too. There was a suggestive comment by George Cumberland on 24 August 1820: 'Mrs Hanning (Molly Anning) is the dealer at Lyme. Col Birch is generally at Charmouth (they say *Miss Anning attends him).*' [13] Another possible partner was Henry De la Beche: their hypothetical relationship is the subject of a novel by Sheila Cole *The Dragon in the Cliff* (1993): certainly they remained friends throughout her life, and he paid her warm tribute when she died.

More solid and more tantalizing are some references in the Journals of Anna Maria Pinney. On 8 November 1831 she wrote

> Been out yesterday and today with Mary Anning fossilizing. Miss Lucy Oakes went with us today ... As soon as she left us Mary Anning turned round to me and said 'That young lady

> has been crossed in love'. This woman must have penetration to have discovered such a thing without any conversation except on Geology. [14]

At the time Mary Anning herself was apparently undergoing a prolonged emotional crisis. On 23 January 1832 Anna Maria Pinney wrote of her

> Her wonderful history (which I cannot consider myself at liberty even to write) interested me ... I felt the power of the motions by which she was actuated, and I should have been glad to have possessed sufficient strength of mind to have done the same. An illness of eight years could not bend that spirit, though acute pain supplied the place of health, the bodily anguish was small with what must have been suffered by a proud mind, who had hoped from childhood to see herself removed from her low situation in life, and suddenly saw those hopes blasted by Satanic treachery.[15]

But in the same entry Anna Maria Pinney reported Mary's mother as saying 'her Mary had no sweethearts, and she did not suppose that she went talking about that there nonsense to Miss Pinney.' On 19 February 1832 Anna Maria Pinney added

> ... Heard from Mary Anning - poor thing - she feels the misery of her hardened heart and almost fears the door of mercy shut ...[16]

It is hard to know what to make of this story, but it certainly looks as if it was she, as much as Lucy Oakes, who had been crossed in love, and this had provoked some of the black and violent moods on which several commented. She could thus have lost the opportunity to escape from domestic difficulties and privations. Any idea of reaching the easy and promised land in which her visitors so carelessly lived could have receded like a mirage.

The 1820s and 1830s saw real poverty in Dorset of a kind we now tend to associate with Bangladesh or Africa south of the Sahara. The majority of the population worked on the land, and depending on the weather and the vagaries of food supply lived close to the margin of subsistence. There were no social safety nets except poor relief, and few had savings to protect themselves from disaster. The

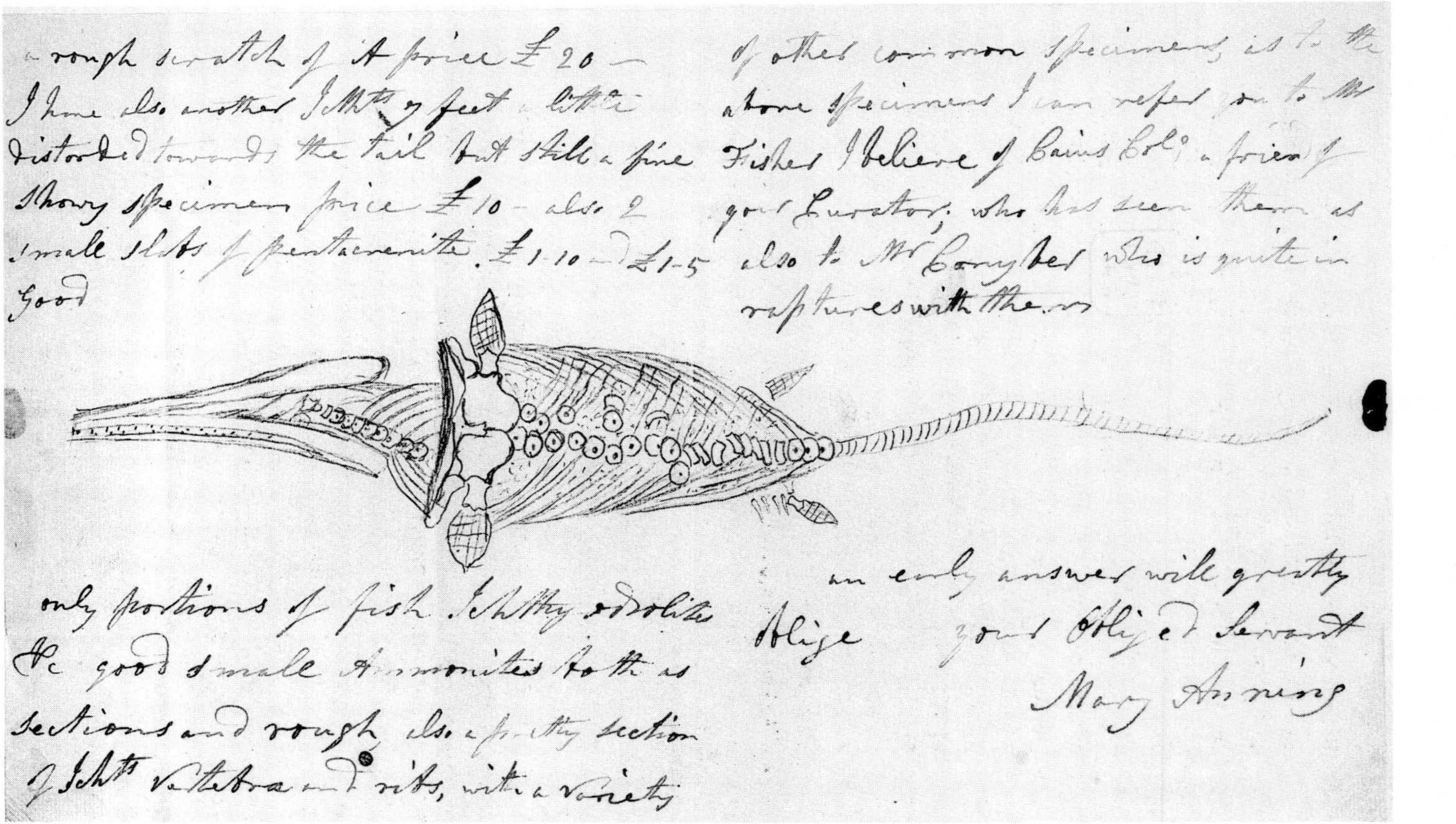
a rough scratch of it price £20 —
I have also another Ichth^s 7 feet a little
distorted towards the tail but still a fine
showy specimen price £10 – also 2
small slabs of pentacrenite £1-10 and £1-5
Good

only portions of fish Ichthyodorulites
&c good small Ammonites both as
sections and rough also a pretty section
of Ichth^s vertebra and ribs, with a variety

of other common specimens as to the
above specimens I can refer you to Mr
Fisher I believe of Caius Coll. a friend of
your Curator, who has seen them as
also to Mr Conybeare who is quite in
raptures with them

an early answer will greatly
oblige your Obliged Servant
Mary Anning

Part of a letter from Mary Anning to Dean Sedgwick, 4 May 1843. The letter, from the Adam Sedgwick collection, is reproduced by kind permission of the Syndics of Cambridge University Library.

result was occasional famine, a severely undernourished population and occasional riots of the kind which Richard Anning led in 1800. The disparity between the incomes of labourers and even artisans and those of the gentry and upwards was vast: comparisons in money terms are always misleading, but the price of one of Mary Anning's fossils, even when the fashion for them diminished in the 1830s, could have kept a family going for a year or more, and must often have done so.

Mary Anning had brains and skill as well as luck. Her list of significant discoveries, between the Ichthyosaur which her brother Joseph and she put together in 1811 to 1812, to her last major find of a Plesiosaur - *Plesiosaurus macrocephalus* - in 1830, is impressive by any reckoning. In earlier or later times she would not have had the same impulse to discover, and the impact of her discoveries would have been much less. The list includes at least three complete Ichthyosaurs (1818, 1821 and 1830), two Plesiosaurs (1823 and 1830), a quantity of coprolites from 1824 onwards which she correctly identified as fossil faeces, a fine specimen of the cephalopod *Belemnosepia* (1828) complete with its supply of fossil ink (which her friend Elizabeth Philpot used for sketching), at least one Pterodactyl (1828), and the fossil fish *Squaloraja* (1828), then interpreted as a transition between the shark and the ray. Many but not all of these specimens still exist. To them should be added quantities of ammonites, brittle star fish and other marine fossils. Whatever others may have found then and since, Mary Anning remains without peer as the prime collector of Lyme Regis.

What were her special strengths? First she had the sharpest eyes in the business. She saw what others failed to see, and almost like a water diviner could tell the presence of a fossil from the merest knob on the surface. She had immense patience and persistence, and from experience knew when as well as where to look. She was out in all weathers, and physically courageous and tough (Anna Maria Pinney records being picked up and carried by her 'with the same ease as you would a baby'). Once a fossil had been located, she took extraordinary pains in extracting or directing its extraction without damaging it.

Yet perhaps her greatest skill was in putting the pieces of a fossil specimen together. As Lady Silvester recorded on 17 September 1824, when Mary was 25:

> ... the extraordinary thing in this young woman is that she has made herself so thoroughly acquainted with the science that the moment she finds any bones she knows to what tribe they belong. She fixes the bones on a frame with cement and then makes drawings and has them engraved ...[17]

George Roberts made the same point in the 1834 edition of his *History of Lyme Regis* when he referred to her 'great judgement in extracting the animals, and infinite skill and manipulation in their development.' Indeed her record in the accurate reassembly of fossils remains second to none. It indicates that she had the rare gift of understanding their anatomy: in short how the creatures of the Lower Jurassic actually worked. The quality of her reconstructions added greatly to their public impact. The collector Thomas Hawkins went into rhapsodies. William Buckland, who described her specimen of a Pterodactyl in 1829, found it like one of the 'dragons of romance and heraldry'.

Thus Mary Anning uncovered a brave new world, or rather a very old one. What that world had been, and how it should be understood, was the central conundrum of the first half of the nineteenth century. Geology was then the queen of the sciences. It occupied the kind of place in people's minds as evolution and natural selection did in the second half of the century, physics in the first half of the twentieth, and information technology with molecular genetics in our own times. Perhaps the single most important change was the growing realization of what has rightly been called deep time. It was James Hutton who in 1795 set out the notion of a seamless continuity of present and past in a world in which 'we find no vestige of a beginning, - no prospect of an end'.

It is all but impossible for us to think our way back into the minds of those who conducted, often in ferocious language, the controversies which this intellectual revolution initiated. Of course they constitute only a tiny minority, and their influence took time to spread. For most people at the end of the eighteenth century the Bible was a record, derived from God, of the creation and history of the Earth. Much ingenious effort had been put into calculation of the time span which was at most a few thousand years. Since then there had been such catastrophes or discontinuities as the Flood.

It is not surprising that the first reaction of many - in particular her friend Buckland - was to try and reconcile the written account in the Bible with the new and different evidence from the rocks. To think otherwise risked discrediting, or at least making metaphorical, the Bible itself. That scarcely worried such geologists as Charles Lyell who in a letter of 5 November 1830, wrote that the real purpose of his book *Principles of Geology* was 'to sink the diluvialists, and in short all the theological sophists'.[18] It would be a mistake to categorize too sharply the different schools which grew up. Vulcanists, who believed the earth was born from volcanoes, and Neptunists, who believed that it had crystallized from a primordial ocean, changed and qualified their views as time went on. The same is true of the catastrophists, who, often with a theological agenda, saw the history of the earth as a series of catastrophes; and the uniformitarians who saw it in terms of slow indeterminate changes or cycles over immeasurable time. As Gillispie has commented:

> If Buckland feared that without cataclysms there was no God, Lyell was as fundamentally apprehensive, lest, without uniformity, there would be no science.[19]

Looking back over these, as so many other disputes, in retrospect, it is hard to avoid the conclusion that nearly all were right and nearly all were wrong. By the end of Mary Anning's life in 1847, the uniformitarians were in broad ascendancy among the learned and educated. Darwin's work on the gradual evolution of living species followed logically on a long view of the physical history of the Earth.

Mary Anning must have been aware of these continuing controversies, not least because she knew personally most of those involved. We do not know how much Buckland, De la Beche, Murchison, Sedgwick, Conybeare and others confided in her and conveyed to her their enthusiasm, but some of them worked with her on the scientific detail and certainly made use of her knowledge (for example Buckland over her identification of coprolites). Did they discuss with her the physiology of the Ichthyosaur or of the Pterodactyl, as eloquently described by Buckland in his Bridgewater

Treatise of 1836? Or that of the cephalopod *Belemnosepia* with its bounteous fossil ink? There is evidence to suggest that Henry De la Beche's gory illustration of life in ancient Dorset *(Duria Antiquior)* was inspired by her work and was for her financial benefit.[20]

We have only one or two fragments to point to what was going on in her mind. In a letter to Mrs Solly on 10 June 1844, she wrote

> ... from what little I have seen of the fossil World and Natural History, I think the connection or analogy between the Creatures of the former and present World excepting as to size, much greater than is generally supposed....[21]

There is an undated and unsigned memorandum in Mary Anning's handwriting, now in the Richard Owen correspondence in the Natural History Museum in London. It was among the Anning papers sold to the Earl of Enniskillen by Mary Anning's nephew Albert Anning on 13 August 1885. It is a call for caution in comparing fossil species and existing ones, and carries a strong implication that fossil species could become extinct (a major point in the controversies of the time). Thus

> The family of ammonites ... contains more than two hundred fossil species according to many authors, and it does not seem possible to reduce this estimate above one half; yet of all those not one is known recent, and the only recent species of the whole genus is a very minute shell; yet the fossil species sometimes measures three feet in diameter ... the same remarks will apply to the belemnites of which no recent species is known ....

It continues in the same vein on 'marine oviparous quadrupeds', fossil crocodiles and even animals from the most recent strata 'mingled in the diluvial detritus' ...

> M Cuvier has shown at large the little probability there is that any of them exist in an unknown condition. It must be carefully remembered that an accurate and vigorous knowledge of zoology is required in any one who ventures to discuss the subject; a superficial acquaintance with it can only lead into confusion and error.[22]

This memorandum, whether copied or composed by Mary

Anning, brings out two important points: her interest in the science and her understanding of it; and her caution over reaching premature conclusions. Many such were of course being drawn at the time, the most notorious being in a book published anonymously in 1844 entitled *Vestiges of Creation* by Robert Chambers. It was universally condemned (not least for its views on evolution of species) but it was as universally read.

So far as is known, Mary Anning only visited London once - in July 1829 - when she stayed with the Murchisons. Her account of it is now in the Richard Owen archive. It contains observations on what she saw at the Geological Society, including a fossil specimen of a Plesiosaur she found hardly distinguishable from one of her own discoveries. For the rest her account is full of wonder at the buildings, libraries and historical relics of London.[23]

Most of the other papers in the collection were dispersed or have disappeared. Among the survivors, apparently in Mary Anning's handwriting, is a satirical poem *The Complaint of a sunbeam against Dr Faraday,* and another *Encomium Murchisonaum* in praise of her friend Sir Roderick Murchison. Here are some verses from it which recall her taste for an opposition among big-wigs:

> ... Let Sedgwick say how things began
> Defend the old Creation plan
> And smash the new one, - if he can, -
> Sir Roderick
>
> Let Buckland set the land to rights,
> Find meat in peas, and starch in blights,
> And future food in coprolites,
> Sir Roderick
>
> Let Agassiz appreciate tails,
> And like the Virgin hold the scales,
> And Owen draw the teeth of whales
> Sir Roderick
>
> Take then thy orders hard to spell,
> And titles more than man can spell. -
> I wish all such were earn'd so well
> Sir Roderick [24]

As Murchison was not knighted until 1846, this poem must have been copied only months before Mary Anning died.

One of her commonplace books and part of another have also survived. She had by then abandoned her dissenting past and joined the Church of England. The first book contains copies of prayers and some verse; and the second some loose sheets on which are written in her handwriting copies of hymns, verses, *Moral Maxims* from Mrs Seward's *Letters*, and a couple of articles, one on Woman and the other on the planets. They do not add much to knowledge about her.[25]

Her last years were sad. Interest in fossils had declined, and she had made no more big discoveries. At the same time she must have enjoyed the recognition which came to her. Following the meeting of the British Association for the Advancement of Science in Dublin in 1835, £200 was raised for her by private subscription. In 1838 her friend Buckland apparently managed to persuade the Prime Minister Lord Melbourne to add £300. Together these sums yielded her an annuity of £25. In 1846, when it was known that she was ill, the members of the Geological Society of London organized another private subscription. So although her income was not large, she was not in want.

By then she was dying. Her mother Molly, with whom she had lived and remained close to all her life, died in 1842. In 1845 she found that she was suffering from breast cancer, and it was from this that she died in Lyme on 9 March 1847. Her brother Joseph died just over two years later. They share a tombstone in the yard by the church overlooking the blue waters of Lyme Bay.

What then was she like as a person? In the words of her mother, 'she was a history and a mystery'. Certainly she became history in herself, and to her contemporaries she was a continuing mystery'. How could she have combined so much: the little girl struck by lightning, the discerning collector, the anatomist of a long distant world, the shrewd business woman, the friend of the great and learned, the proud and unyielding spirit? Perhaps most telling was the opinion of the local people whence she came. Their repeated testimony is of a kind, straightforward and generous person, who did her best for them at all times. Long afterwards Gulielma Lister recorded a local recollection of her.

> She were good to the poor, she were; whenever she found a little cag (keg) on the shore, she would cover it up, and not let the preventitive men see it, but would tell some poor person of it. [26]

From another social perspective Anna Maria Pinney wrote in her journal on 23 January 1832

> ... she is gentle, attentive and has a simple ... way of expressing her affectionate feelings, beyond any person I ever met with ... she will attend the sick poor night and day, when they are ill with infectious diseases, she has supported her mother and brother in bitter poverty and (even) when she was so ill that she was ... brought fainting from the Beach. [27]

In memoirs published at the end of the century, Nellie Waring (or Sister Emma) remembered visiting her and her mother in their shop:

> There lived this very timid, very unpretending, very patient and very celebrated woman, the discoverer of the Ichthyosaurus and of other fossil remains which were living animals before the Deluge. We, as children, had large dealings with Miss Anning, our pocket-money was freely spent on the little ammonites which she washed and burnished till they shone like metal.... She would see to us with the sweetest temper, bearing with all our little fancies and never finding us too troublesome as we turned over her trays of curiosities, and concluded by spending a few pence only, and this we might do as often as we liked without offence. She must have been poor enough, for her little shop was scantily furnished, and her own dress always of the very plainest, she was very thin and had a high forehead, and large eyes which seemed to me to have a kindly consideration for her little customers. [28]

In fact we know relatively little about her personal appearance. She lived before the age of photography, and the famous oil painting of her, now in the Natural History Museum in London, has an artificial air. But it did not try to prettify her, and as it seems to have

A water-colour sketch of Mary Anning at work on the beach, reproduced from the original in a private collection by kind permission of the owner.

been painted in her life time (the artist, apparently a Mr Grey, submitted it without success to the Royal Academy for exhibition in February 1842) it probably does bear some resemblance to her. Another similar portrait was painted in pastel by B J M Donne three years after her death. More realistic was an undated water colour sketch or caricature which shows her from behind as a stout, somewhat masculine figure with heavy petticoat below check skirt, clogs, battered top hat (perhaps a kind of prototype safety helmet), and geological hammer on the Lyme beaches.[29]

It is no wonder that even in her life time Mary Anning was the stuff of legend. As Hugh Torrens has remarked, she has inspired cartoons since 1830, poetry (or verse) since 1838, literature since 1951 and 1969, novels (particularly for children) since 1966, television since the 1970s, dance since 1987, and film since 1982 (if as seems likely she had something in common with *The French Lieutenant's Woman* in John Fowles's famous book and film). She has been enlisted in many causes, from science to feminism, and is now what she was in her lifetime, a boon to the tourist industry. A stained glass window in her honour was installed in Lyme church within three years of her death. She even has a road named after her. Of the verses which may be related to her, the most famous is the tongue twister song by Terry Sullivan in 1908:

> She sells sea-shells on the sea-shore,
> The shells she sells are sea-shells, I'm sure,
> For if she sells sea-shells on the sea-shore,
> Then I'm sure she sells sea-shore shells.

More personal were J W Preston's lines in 1884

> Miss Anning, as a child, ne'er passed
> A pin upon the ground;
> But picked it up, and so at last
> An Ichthyosaurus found.[30]

Perhaps the most curious product of her fame was a probable representation of her as one of a pair of ceramic nodding figurines about $5^1/_4$ inches high manufactured in Germany between 1861 and 1887. She carries chisel and basket, and her companion, so far unidentified, carries tools as well. Could he have been her brother Joseph, or conceivably Henry De la Beche? It is nice to think of them nodding together.* [31]

It fell to Henry De la Beche to pay Mary Anning an unprecedented tribute the year after her death. For reason of her sex apart from anything else, she could never have been a Fellow of the Geological Society, still less a Fellow of the Royal Society. But in his Presidential Address to the Geological Society in 1848 De la Beche said

> ... I cannot close this notice of our losses by death without adverting to that one, who though not placed among even the easier classes of society, but one who had to earn her daily bread by her labour, yet contributed by her talents and untiring researches in no small degree to our knowledge of the great Enalio-Saurians, and other forms of organic life entombed in the vicinity of Lyme Regis....

He went on to speak of her skill in developing the skeletons of Ichthyosaurs and Plesiosaurs 'which without her care would never have been presented to the comparative anatomists in the uninjured form so desirable for their examination'.[32]

If Mary Anning has become an Icon, she fully deserves it. But Icons need definition. She was no dainty heroine from children's tales, no conventional creature of fantasy, no mere local prodigy, no defender of women' rights, no prettified hand maiden of science. Instead she was a tough, practical, complex, generous, sometimes prickly, independent-minded person of great intelligence, who surmounted the obstacles of her sex and circumstances to help lay the foundations of a new science of the earth.

* These figurines have recently (December 1995) been most generously donated to the Philpot Museum by their owner, author of the article. [31]

References

1. Mantell MSS, Alexander Turnbull Library, Wellington, New Zealand: Quoted by Torrens BSHS lecture 1993 p 4
2. De la Beche correspondence National Museum of Wales: quoted by W D Lang in 'Mary Anning's Escape From Lightning': *Proceedings of the Dorset Natural History & Archaeological Society* vol 80:1959 pp 91-2
3. See note 2 above: p 92
4. Journals of Anna Maria Pinney 1831-3: quoted by W D Lang in 'Mary Anning and Anna Maria Pinney': *Proceedings of the Dorset Natural History & Archaeological Society* Vol 76: 1956 pp 146-7
5. *Bristol Mirror* 11 January 1823: quoted by Torrens BSHS lecture 1993 p 6
6. Journal of Thomas Allan 25 June 1824: quoted by W D Lang in 'Mary Anning of Lyme' *Natural History Magazine* No 34 Vol V p 75
7. E Welch 'Lady Silvester's tour through Devonshire in 1824' *Devon and Cornwall Notes and Queries 1967:* quoted by Torrens BSHS lecture 1993 p 8
8. *The Journal of Gideon Mantell:* ed E Cecil Chewell Oxford 1940 p 108
9. C G Carns: *The King of Saxony's Journey through England and Scotland in the year 1844:* quoted by Torrens BSHS lecture 1993 p 11
10. See note 4 above: p 147
11. See note 4 above: p 150
12. See note 4 above: p 147
13. Bristol Library MSS 36520: quoted by Torrens BSHS lecture 1993 p 5
14. See note 4 above: p 148
15. See note 4 above: p 148
16. See note 4 above: p 149
17. See note 7 above: p 8
18. Gillispie *Genesis & Geology* 1970 p 133
19. Gillispie p 121
20. See note 1 above: Torrens 1993 p 10

21. Quoted by W D Lang in 'Mary Anning and the Fire at Lyme in 1844': *Proceedings of the Dorset Natural History and Archaeological Society* vol 74: 1953 p 175
22. Richard Owen Correspondence: General Library Natural History Museum vol 1 pp 149-50
23. See note 22 above: pp 153-4
24. See note 22 above: pp 151-2
25. W D Lang in 'More About Mary Anning, Including a Newly Found Letter': *Proceedings of the Dorset Natural History and Archaeological Society* vol 71: 1949 p 188
26. Lister's Thesaurus quoted by W D Lang: see note 25 above: pp 187-8
27. See note 4 above: p 148
28. S E (Sister Emma Waring): *Peeps Into an Old Playground: Memoirs of the Past* 1895: quoted by W D Lang: see note 25 above: p 187
29. W D Lang: 'Portraits of Mary Anning and Other Items': *Proceedings of the Dorset Natural History Museum and Archaeological Society* vol 81: 1959 pp 89-91; and see note 25 above: p 187
30. See note 25 above: p 186
31. Hilma R Irtz: 'Mary Anning' in *Antiques and Collecting* September 1994
32. See note 6 above: pp 80-1

Reading List

W D LANG

'Mary Anning of Lyme, Collector and Vendor of Fossils, 1799 - 1847': *Natural History Magazine* No 34 Vol V 1936

A series of articles published in the *Proceedings of the Dorset Natural History and Archaeological Society:* Vol 60 (1939), Vol 62 (1941), Vol 66 (1944), Vol 68 (1947), Vol 71 (1949), Vol 74 (1953), Vol 76 (1956), Vol 80 (1959) and Vol 81 (1959)

HUGH TORRENS

'Mary Anning (1799 - 1847)': Presidential Address to the British Society for the History of Science: April 1993; published in the *British Journal for the History of Science,* Vol 28 pp 257-284, 1995

(with MICHAEL A TAYLOR) 'Saleswoman to a New Science: Mary Anning and the Fossil Fish Squaloraja from the Lias of Lyme Regis': *Proceedings of the Dorset Natural History and Archaeological Society:* Vol 108 (1986)

J M EDMONDS

'The Fossil Collection of the Misses Philpot of Lyme Regis': *Proceedings of the Dorset Natural History and Archaeological Society:* Vol 98 (1976)

A HALLAM

Great Geological Controversies: Oxford: 1983 and 1989

CHARLES COULSTON GILLISPIE

Genesis and Geology: Harvard University Press: 1951, and Harper and Row (New York) 1959

NICOLAAS A RUPKE

The Great Chain of History: Oxford 1983 and 1986

ed W S McKERROW
The Ecology of Fossils: Duckworth 1978

LYNN BARBER
The Heyday of Natural History: Jonathan Cape 1980

ROSAMOND WOLFF PURCELL and STEPHEN JAY GOULD
Finders, Keepers: W W Norton (New York) 1992 and Pimlico (London) 1993

MARTIN J S RUDWICK
The Great Devonian Controversy: University of Chicago Press: 1985